TRAPPED IN TWO WORLDS
MY DARKEST DREAMS

Written and Illustrated

by

MARIA PALOMINO

Edited by Lori Shriner, Firewataer Creative

INTRODUCTION

Since she was a little girl, Maria Palomino always had weird dreams. Dreams about being somewhere else – often very far away – fighting or running from monsters and strange people. Yet, Maria found her dreams would become adventures. Every time she fell asleep, she felt like a traveler journeying to her past with people she met along the road of her life. It felt like another world altogether. Every door in her dreams opened a new and different place to explore, where even speaking another language was easy. The dreams may seem weird or even scary… but Maria is a fighter who defeats the demons within them. Because her world of dreams is as real to her as waking life, Maria feels called to share these experiences with her readers. She is sure that many others have similar dreams and can also share the ability to remember every detail. Maria is not the only person who lives in two worlds.

DESPERATE TO FIND MY FATHER

10/18/2010

It was a windy afternoon. The grass was green and wet. The sky was clear blue, but there were dark clouds. They were getting darker and moving fast. I found myself standing in my parents' living room, looking through the second story window. I was watching Mother Nature destroying everything in her path with her greatest power. The beautiful, colorful flowers my mother had on the balcony of the second story were flying around in circles along with other debris. The wind was getting stronger and making a furious tornado. I couldn't believe my eyes! It was moving so fast.

I wanted to go out and find my father, but I couldn't go. I felt insecure about being outside and not finding him. I turned my head to look inside but no one was around. The living room was empty. Next door, the kitchen was empty and I couldn't imagine where my family had gone. It was getting darker in the house. The tornado was taking over. The windows sounded like they were going to break at any moment and let the howling wind inside.

I touched a window and thought about my dad. Where could he be right now? As I walked to the stairs on my way out, I saw some kids playing on the steps. My mom was now in the empty kitchen, cooking. She asked me if I was ready to eat and asked if I could find my father to tell him the food was ready. I saw my dad on the balcony sitting in a chair, drinking beer. I felt happy, as if I had woken from the nightmare, but was still dreaming.

As I got close to my father, he was moving further away. I tried to reach out to him, but a truck stopped in front of my house. A couple of men came out with guns, shooting at my father until he fell to the ground. I felt desperation and panic like never before. They were killing him in front of my eyes! I ran fast to beg my father to stay alive. I sat next to him to hold him in my arms and tell him I loved him with all my heart. He suddenly disappeared. I couldn't find him anywhere.

My heart was racing. I ran out of my house and saw a couple of horses on the side of the road. I grabbed one and jumped on his back. I rode to see if I could catch the guys who shot my dad. I rode everywhere to ask if anyone had seen them, but nobody knew who or where they were. My body was getting tired and so was the horse, so I decided to head home.

As I was riding on the side of the road, I saw my dad walking in front of me. He was going toward our house. I told the horse to speed up. My father was alive and I had to reach him!

I finally got there and said thank you to the beautiful horse. My father and I walked side by side. I felt very happy it was a dream, but it was still a dream I had to wake up from.

ANGRY OCEAN

12/25/2004

I found myself hanging out in a small, white apartment that had a backyard leading to the ocean and the front door to the city streets. There was a table for four people to eat at right off the living room. I saw a couple of friends sitting there, just chilling. Suddenly, someone ran inside from the front door and said to me, "Let's hurry and go for a walk. It's cloudy outside and looks like it's about to rain." I went out through the front door with him and started walking south from the apartment down the highway. As we walked, we were talking about somebody who was in jail and decided to visit him.

When we arrived, there was a line of people waiting to see their loved ones. The line moved a little slow and I was tired of having to stand, but we finally got to a big office. They had wooden benches to sit on until they called your name. I saw a lot of police officers sitting across a long, big desk working hard and checking the status of visitor driver licenses to get them in to see their loved ones.

They called our name and we got up from the bench. We walked toward the big desk, and they asked us to leave our belongings. We followed the rules, and then walked deep into the jail cells. While my friend was ready to see his friend, a random guy managed to grab a gun and started shooting at the sky. We got on our knees and waited for the guy to leave. The police officers almost confused us for the shooter.

We saw an open door and ran out. It led to the backyard of the jail, where we saw giant silver fences that would be hard to jump over. An officer joined us to escape because it was getting crazy in there. He cut the fences for us, but we couldn't leave. I looked at a pool of trapped water that grew into a big lake from heavy rains that afternoon. We were expecting rain, but not like that; it was such a hard rain that we saw sharks waiting for us to jump in and eat us alive. I wasn't scared at all. My confidence led me to jump in first and calmly swim to the north side of the jail. My friend and the policeman did the same, following me. Sharks were swimming next to me. The policeman was dragged down into the water. I touched the water's edge and got out, but what a surprise! I had landed in the backyard of my friend's apartment.

I opened the back door and told everyone what was happening. We opened the front door to see how high the water was on the streets and found our side was dry. We walked to a store near us and I saw people running for their lives, headed west.

We looked back and saw an enormous wave coming right at us. My first reaction was, "Oh noooo tsunami, here I go again!" I held my breath and waited for it since I couldn't run anywhere. I felt the clear water wash over me. The force of it was strong, taking everything in its path. I didn't lose my hope, so I calmly waited underwater for the wave to pass.

It happened fast, and then I opened my eyes and swam until I touched the ground.

I looked up and the sky looked like a tornado was coming. More waves would come. I looked at the ocean and saw things floating and falling into the water. Mountains disappeared within the waves. Only half of the mountain range was still visible. Finally, some dry land appeared. I stood up and walked toward my friend's apartment, but there wasn't much left of it. Water got inside and the rest was gone, including a few of the houses down the street.

I turned west to head far from the ocean. I couldn't walk fast because my body was so tired from swimming. As I walked, I saw some girl sitting and helping people. Others were in search of food, it was crazy. Suddenly I looked and saw the waves coming again. I could see them growing larger and angrier, so once again I held my breath and let myself into the water. The first wave came fast, and I saw buildings sinking. I swam back to shore again but the journey felt longer. The ocean took the city with it, and I could only see a mountain very far in the distance.

I swam until I touched ground. The water was up to my knees. I walked along and found a couple of old people hiding under a piece of aluminum siding they used to protect themselves. This was not going to help them; the waves took half the city, and could destroy anything. It started raining. I saw a house next to them, the only house left. I tried to open the door but it was locked. I asked someone to help me. Together, we broke in. Whoa! The house was in perfect condition, despite the storm. Two men and a little girl were living inside, and very frightened of us. I told them we were not dangerous. We needed a place to stay for the night because it was raining, and we didn't know if the waves would come back again. But the waves returned, taking everything with them. I ran farther west where there was nothing but land. Thank God it was just a dream!

UGLY, BLACK, ANGRY SNAKE

12/19/2004

Next to the rolling blue ocean, I see a hotel. It was white with blue trim and was at least four stories tall. Some kids were playing outside and speaking in another language. One of them was my five-year-old son, dressed in a white t-shirt and blue sweat pants. It was great to see him playing with the other kids. My family was with me in the penthouse suite that had a narrow stretch of balcony. Looking down at the ocean, I felt like it would swallow me. Meanwhile, my daughter was in the living room hanging out with a couple of my sisters, and my parents were in the living room waiting for food.

Everything seemed normal until I went out to look for my son. I couldn't go on the balcony because I was afraid I'd slip and fall into the ocean, so I decided to walk downstairs. I saw people running into the hotel, making their way to the street, or just watching it all happen. As I kept walking away the path got muddy, and I noticed a lot of plants that were withered or dying.

It was getting dark. I felt as if someone were following me, and I was too scared to look back. I started running to find my son. The mud started getting thicker and harder to walk through, and tiny black insects began crawling everywhere. I almost stepped on a small snake. I found myself in danger of falling into a river, afraid an alligator would eat me. I could see a few coming with their big mouths open, ready to eat anything that crossed their path. I heard my son's voice. I looked and saw a big, black anaconda snake following a group of kids, my son along with them running for his life.

I got nervous and called out to him, "I will rescue you, don't worry!" I wasn't scared of the big, fat, black snake. As I ran to him, I almost slipped and fell into the river. I reached for the branch of an old, dry tree and held my body against it, but the path was getting worse and small alligators were coming my way. One of the gators ran up behind me to eat me, but I kicked it hard and pushed him away with my foot.

I saw my son hiding in an old mud hut that was too close to the river. I screamed his name until he heard me. I took him in my arms. The big, black snake wrapped around my legs with its strong tail, squeezing me so hard I had to let go of my son so he wouldn't get eaten. I told him to go back to the hotel and wait for me. As he ran away, a couple of kids were eaten by alligators. I got mad and fought the big snake. I heard a helicopter above, searching for us from the blue sky. I wanted to jump into it, but the snake wasn't making it easy so I ran to hide behind another old tree.

There were more houses around, but no one lived in them. It looked like the animals had taken over. I saw the snake looking for me. Many more animals appeared. Oh my God! A spider was close to my hand. At that moment, I realized it was just a dream and wanted to wake up. I was getting nowhere and my only chance of escape was to run fast. I found a few more kids on my way. I carried them, one by one, to a safe place away from the river, and discovered the last child was my son. I carried him to the other side of the river, where we all finally escaped the dangerous animals.

We headed back to the hotel. I saw men at the bar drinking out of crystal glasses. There was green grass and the ocean was calm. People were having fun. I was tired and went inside. Holding my son close. I walked all the way up to my room where our family was. They were wondering where we had been. As I tried to explain, I looked down from the balcony and saw the big, black snake now in the ocean coming toward the hotel. I quickly closed all the doors, but found another snake in my daughter's room trying to eat her! I grabbed her and took her from the room, closed the door, and woke up.

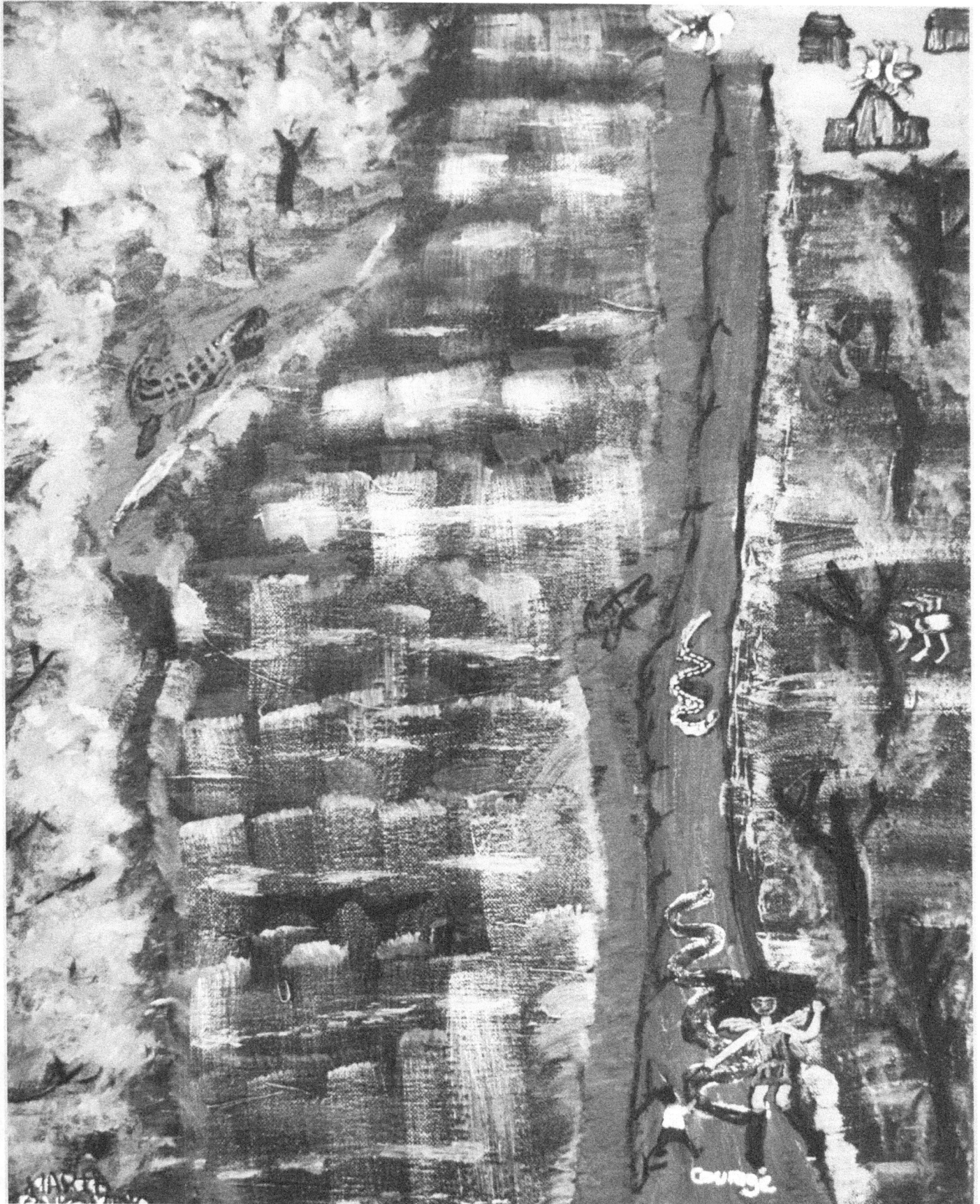

MIXED-UP DREAM

9/16/2012

I was walking on a mountain made of white sand. It had dirt roads everywhere, and a few houses around. Down the road, I saw a few pools of water. As I walked deep into the mountains it started to get dark and scary. The moon hid behind the clouds and I could barely see around me. Suddenly, a black car made in the '50s passed me by with a couple inside. I was heading to my sister's house, but it was far away from familiar roads. The car stopped and a girl asked me why I was taking too long to get there.

I was confused, but I got in the car because the girl's face was familiar to me. I sat next to a baby drinking a bottle of milk. In the other seat was a little girl that was my daughter. What a surprise! I asked her what she was doing there. She said she was looking for our dog because it ran away. This made me so sad because I loved my dog! I looked out the windows to see if I could find him, but nothing was there except the road and trees. The baby started crying, annoying the other passengers. The man driving told the girl to shut up the baby but she couldn't. I was just there watching, feeling helpless because I couldn't touch the baby. I was not sure why.

The man and the girl started arguing. The man struggled to gain control of the car as he let go of the wheel to beat her up. Suddenly, through the front windshield, I saw my dog walking close to a house. My heart beat faster as the man and girl kept fighting. The car crashed, landing close to where my dog was. I got out to see if he was alive. I took him in my arms and carried him to the house.

My daughter was in the car with the baby, the couple still fighting. The man grabbed a gun and started shooting at his girlfriend. I ran back to the car to get my daughter and the baby out, but the man pointed the gun at my chest and told me to leave them in there. I told him I just wanted my daughter and the baby out of the car. He backed up the car and drove away with them still inside.

I went to the house to check on my dog. He was still moving. Then I picked up a phone and dialed 911. No one was answering, but I kept trying. I thought I should go out and find a police officer because it was better than calling and getting no answer. I looked down the road and saw an old officer walking near a pool hall. I ran down the hill to speak with him, but I couldn't get anywhere. The more I wanted to be there, the slower I ran. My legs were heavy and tired.

I saw a man who looked like a hillbilly walking to his big truck. I asked him if I could use his truck to find the man who took the girls and left one for dead on the side of the road. He told me the guy was inside the house next door. We walked to the house but found nothing. We broke in just as the man was going to shoot the baby. I woke up at that moment… damn it!

DESPERATE DREAM OR NIGHTMARE?

11/17/2013

There was a lot of traffic waiting on the white concrete city streets. I drove deeper into it and found blocks of houses that led up to a small mountain. Old people lived in all the houses. I saw them walking outside very slowly. Driving away from the traffic toward the houses, I saw a small, old shopping plaza with only two businesses open- a grocery store and a launderette.

I drove my car and kept looking around. I saw a big library in front of the traffic-filled streets. With me was my daughter and a baby, but I only have one daughter in real life. This child was very cute, and I loved him. Every time I looked at him in the back seat, it reminded me of someone but I didn't know who. Finally the traffic moved, and I stopped in the library to get something. I ran in and out fast. I saw that my car was gone with the children inside.

I walked around but found nothing. I wanted to call the police, but they were already there. I asked one of them to help me. He said, "We have your children, your car, and your house." This officer was really mad.

I said, "Why? I haven't done anything bad. Give me back my things, or I will call my lawyer!" He walked to a car that looked like mine, where another police officer was sitting inside.

I got in the car with the officer and he asked me in a French accent, "Where is your friend, bitch? We know you have him!" I got very angry and didn't say a word. I had my phone in my hand and was thinking about calling some real police and a lawyer, but I still felt I had not done anything wrong. How can these people be so cruel to me?

The officers let me drive. In the car were clothes for the children I thought I had left in my other car. For a moment, it seemed like this was my own car, but no; my car was automatic, and this one had a stick shift. I stopped the car immediately and told them, "This is not my car, you bitches! Give me back my children and things now!" They started laughing. I got out of the car and ran up to the houses in the mountains where there was a lady dressed in pajamas. They were white with flowers on them. I knew her! I asked where they took my children. I needed help and asked if she could hide me in her house. She closed the door in my face.

I felt desperate, crying and screaming for help on the street. One lady took my hand and pulled me inside her home. Her house had several mirrors and a large glass door.

She told me, "I know who has them, they are with my husband and not planning to give them back to you unless you tell them where he is hiding." I didn't know where he was or what was going on. I called my lawyer but he said he was busy and hung up on me. I tried to think of who else could help me.

I begged the woman out of desperation to go and find them. In front of her house, the officer with the French accent came along with some other officers to try and get into the house. The lady let them in. I felt sad and cried. I told the officer with the accent, "I have powers, and if you don't give me back my children, I will curse you with my own hands!" I put my hands on his head and said something in French.

He got scared and one of the officers said, "Okay, here are your children. But please tell me where he is."

I showed them the text messages in my phone and told him, "I don't want to hurt you, and I'm not a liar. Here is the proof." He sat on the sofa to read them. At that moment, my two children appeared and I hugged them tight. I woke up feeling desperate.

MISSION OF OUR LIFE SAVER

MISSION OF ONE LIFESAVER

06/28/13

It was during the day, somewhere in the city. The streets looked worn in front of the hotel. It was the only building on the block in good condition. Well-dressed employees worked there. I met up with a couple of people in the lobby, but I could not remember their faces exactly. However, the only thing I can't forget was the word that was mentioned by everyone. They all told me to get a liver. That was my mission.

It was hard for me to get the liver. I would have to take it from someone who was the worst guy on the planet. But if I didn't get it in time, my tall, black friend was going to die. I went to Mexico to deliver the liver. I crossed a street and was instantly there. I got to a house with a rusty-colored wood fence outside. I tried to break in. When I finally make it inside, I see the liver on a plate drowned in blood. I just took it with me and looked at it in my hands. I felt so strange about it all. The liver was still alive! I could feel its warmth. However, I put it in my purse and ran to open the door.

As I opened the door to go outside, I found myself in the hotel I saw earlier. I was looking for my friend to give him the liver but didn't find him anywhere. I went outside, and as I crossed the street there were some guys chasing me around in a big, black suburban. They were driving so fast and close, I almost got hit. I jumped to the other side of the street. Then I saw my tall, black friend crossing the street with another man.

I walked fast toward my friend. Then I took the liver out of my purse and handed it to him; to my surprise, he didn't want it anymore! Across the street were the men with guns, still chasing me. They looked pretty scary. At first, their faces appeared normal but then twisted into hairy, beast-like monsters. At that moment, I told my friend to run with the liver and put it in to save his life. If not, the bad guys would take it from me and he would die. I didn't want that to happen to him.

He took the liver and put it into a hole in his body. All the bad guys disappeared, even the one who stole my friend's liver to begin with. I felt happy he didn't die and he thanked me for saving his life.

EVIL SPIRIT

08/24/2008

I am looking for someone in the city. There is a desperate feeling I cannot find who I am searching for. I saw people selling fruit on the street corners and customers dressed in '80s clothes.

I saw happy people, but felt so strange in this small city. As I turn around, I saw large, old houses with big porches and ceiling fans running. It was a little hot on the streets. I stopped to talk with a blond girl and her boyfriend about how darkness would take over the beautiful city.

I have a flashback. I find myself in a bus with girls and boys ready to go home. The bus driver was eating fruit and driving like a maniac. I took a seat next to a handsome man and gazed into his eyes. I felt I had seen him before, maybe around the neighborhood.

All of a sudden, something happened that made us all run out of the bus. The handsome man ran next to me and I felt protected. We went back to where the dream started. I found an empty house in the corner and walked inside, laying on a bed covered with a white blanket. I stared at the ceiling and saw a big, old black kettle hanging upside down on a wagon wheel with knives and swords on it, ready to fall on top of me.

My body felt possessed. Something was holding me back, I couldn't move or scream but I am not afraid. I felt that God was with me and He would give me the power to fight.

As I felt more trapped, I noticed a man in the corner of the room. He had white skin and long, black hair but his face was not visible. He walked toward me, getting ready to suck my face. I felt his breath on my ear. Suddenly, the window opened and I heard someone scream, "The devil is in my room!"

The man's presence was cold and made my skin crawl with fear. I managed to push him back and yell, "In the name of the Lord of land and King of the universe, let me go!"

As I yelled, some people were trying to open the door. Others were looking in the window. The wind blew inside my room and touched my face. My eyes became paralyzed and I couldn't speak. The handsome man who ran with me earlier kicked in the door, grabbed my arm, and pulled me out of the room. He saved my life and took me away from the evil spirit. We ran outside and I asked someone to go back and kill it. Some people broke into the house and somehow defeated it.

The handsome man and I walked down the street, and we saw people lying on the pavement. They were in a deep, deep sleep. I felt I had found the man I had been looking for since the beginning – I had finally found him – but I was scared because my feelings toward him are not the same. We looked at each other and didn't say much. I wanted to say something, but felt it was too late. Yet, I felt happy someone had defeated the evil spirit that haunted my dream.

FIGHTING CREEPS

11/16/2010

I was sitting on the phone and listening to people talking. My mom is next to me and we are in a stranger's house. The stranger told me one of my brothers moved to a friend's house, and he was happy there. I felt like my heart was beating too fast, ticking like a stopwatch. I was in two places at the same time. The other place was a restaurant that looked more like a school cafeteria. I was with my sister and a couple of friends. Some men started a fight and we wanted to leave. I couldn't open the door. It was very heavy and made of sharp, gray rocks. I stared at a big, green tree outside and thought of my brother. I wanted to see him so badly at that moment.

The door opens and I walk up to a highway not made of concrete. It was long and on each side were tall, green trees. I got in a car and drove until I saw a house that was on the beach. I parked the car and walked fast. At the other place, I hung up the phone and drove with the GPS directing me to the same place- a beach house.

I was anxious and ran in just in time to see a three-year-old kid biting my brother. I couldn't have been more furious! My brother was lying on the floor with blood all over his t-shirt. I grabbed the child's mother and asked her why she let her kid bite my brother. I felt so much anger that I grabbed her shirt and started punching her in the face. I took her outside. That way, her son could see and feel what I was feeling in that moment.

I look outside and see people floating on the ocean in beds like coffins. I could see from where I stood they were all flowing in one direction and many were piling up near the side of the house. The ocean was clear blue. The child grabbed one of the coffin beds and left her there. At that moment, my brother came outside. It was hard for all of us to look at all those dead people floating. It was a very creepy dream.

FLYING OVER THE MOUNTAINS

12/21/2007

I was seated on a big rock, admiring my surroundings in a forest. There was a road between the mountains; it had big pines, brown rocks, clear skies, and a beautiful and clear lake. I could see a few cars driving up to it from afar. It was a calm day.

A Jeep parked next to the rock I was sitting on. There was a tour group at the lake. One man took a camera from a car as another man said, "Film here, and there, and take lots of pictures of it." They took the pictures, walked toward me, and asked me how I was doing. I answered, "Fine, thank you."

Three girls walked by and the men looked at them. One of the guys asked the girls if they wanted to be in a movie they were producing. Right away, the girls told them "Yes! It's so exciting to be in the movies!" One of them started taking off her clothes, and the men told her not to do that. They didn't want to see her body… yet.

Suddenly, I found myself in a room lying on a bed. My sister was trying to wake me up. I heard her voice and got up. I asked her, "Why is it so sad and dark in here?"

"There is a crazy lady outside," she replied. Someone knocked hard on the door and scared us. My sister said, "Come this way. It is a way out to the other side of the house." It looked like a cave crossing, running through the middle of the house. We walked fast until we saw a door at the end of the cave. We opened the door and found ourselves outside in a backyard.

The two film makers were with the girls, around a pool that looked like the same lake I saw in the beginning of the dream. The girls were swimming with a big fish, and there was a small animal I was afraid of. My sister left that place because she said the crazy lady would come there to attack us because she had a virus in her veins. I didn't pay any attention. I was hanging out with all the people at the pool.

The door I came from opened and monkeys started coming out. They were attacking the girls! One of the guys pulled me away toward the pool, but I didn't fall in. Instead, I flew to the top of a tree and watched the monkeys attack everyone. I flew away and landed behind the house I grew up in.

It was getting dark and I walked up to the house, but no one was there. I wondered where everyone had gone. Far away, I saw some people trying to hang a man from a tall, wood pole. I ran over to stop them. I told them to let the guy go free. The man took off so fast, I couldn't see where he went. The group of people became angry and wanted to hang me next for letting him go.

I ran back to my house but didn't want to hide there and get my family in trouble, so I turned left toward the highway and hid next to it. Some friends were walking on the highway and saw me trying to hide. They asked me, "Why are you laying there?" I didn't respond and just flew away.

There was a long, white blanket that blocked the sky. I felt a little trapped and desperate. I decided to walk down to see the other town. The lights from the houses looked pretty. I felt I should leave. I waited for the bus to take me away from there. I spotted a place where the blanket was torn and I slipped out of it to fly away.

I did my best and flew high up, where no one could see me. Passing over the mountains, it was a beautiful view. I crossed over a few towns until I came upon a small village with really nice buildings, colorful lights and green treehouses around it. I landed in the village next to a bridge decorated with white flowers and Christmas lights. I found a green treehouse with a cute little river crossing in front of it. I knocked on the door, a man answered and said, "Welcome to Greenland. You can hide here for a while. We are cartoons!" I really liked it there. I felt safe and secure. I sat on a yellow all-terrain vehicle covered with a green tarp. A lady asked me if I was hungry.

I went outside to explore this wonderful place when I heard a voice calling for help. My reaction was, "Oh no, I have to save him again!" I started to fly, following his voice. I found him and headed back, but I wasn't alone. There were helicopters with soldiers inside flying all around me, trying to catch us. I really didn't know this man well but felt like I had to save him.

I flew faster and higher to get away until I disappeared up into the clouds. I thought no one could defeat me, I was the best at flying! Even the helicopters couldn't catch me. I made it back to Greenland, opened the door to my house and hid him inside. My neighbors complained about it. The soldiers in their helicopters were flying toward the village. The man and I left immediately, and he didn't say a word. On the way, I searched for another place to hide him.

I saw a mountain that looked familiar, so I landed there. Every time I landed, I got this weird feeling in the pit of my stomach that moved up and down; I couldn't control it. Underneath some bushes I found a pillow and a sweater. Someone had slept in there, or lived there. I saw a homeless lady walking toward us. We had to leave. Out of nowhere, some soldiers showed up and told us they weren't going to do us any harm, they wanted to protect us. We walked down the hills with them.

GOD IS ALIVE

10/29/2002

It was an afternoon of pain. I found myself back in my parents' house on the third floor, where a friend was telling me a story about a man I used to know in real life. She said, "I saw him and he asked for you, then he gave me a hug. That was all." When she finished, I decided to look for that man so I asked where he was now. I was going to find him. She showed me the way with her hand and pointed up the mountain.

I couldn't lose any time, so I ran as fast as I could. The only thing I could think of in that moment was that even though I knew I could fly, I was unable to. I tried hard, but I just couldn't do it. I passed by houses made of mud, fields full of corn, and rows of gray stone until I arrived at my destination. From my house, it looked like just a lonely old mountain. As I got closer, I saw houses from my old neighborhood. I saw big trees, more mud houses, dying plants, and people walking around in their everyday routine.

I heard someone scream from far away. I turned my head and saw a little boy in front of my parents' house, trying to get inside. I got scared but yelled down to him, "Stop it! Don't get in my house!" he got mad and yelled back at me in an old man's voice, "I WILL destroy your house!" He started breaking the window on the front door. I ran back to the house and tried to keep the boy from getting in, but his power was so strong I couldn't hold the door by myself. I ran back to the mountain and looked for a place to hide. I saw people running to try and catch me.

It was a cold and cloudy afternoon. The time was passing by, and it was getting dark. I hid underneath a house made of plastic material. People were laying in a bed made of white blankets. I asked one of them where the man was. They said he was there a few minutes ago doing a circus show with some other people. I felt very sad, as though I would never find him. The devil was chasing me and I couldn't leave. People outside were trying to kill me. It seemed like I tried to fight with some of them, but was very tired. I decided to leave.

As soon as I stepped out of the plastic house, a man yelled "Get her!" That man was the devil. I could see him, but others could not because he was wearing a disguise. I ran around a corner and saw a flea market with people buying and selling things. Others were just wandering around. I stopped and looked up. The sky was blue, with very white clouds. I asked God to help me because I felt miserable.

The clouds started moving fast toward me, making the shape of a beautiful dove. The dove then flew to me and said, "Jump on my back. I will help you. On the left side of my wing, I have powder. Throw it at them. It will put them asleep until I take you to your destiny and the man you are looking for." I flew with the dove, and felt like I was flying with God.

I have never felt so alive and loved with the power in my hands. I was excited to get there, so I woke up happy!

34

LATE FOR CLASS

07/28/2013

I was in my room putting on my school uniform as my mom screamed, "Hurry up, get ready or you will be late for your first class!" I went upstairs and took some lunch I thought would be delicious. I put it in my backpack and went outside. My bus stop was on the highway. While I waited, I paced around checking my uniform to make sure it was clean. Blue skirt, white shirt with a tie, white socks. I said to myself, "I look pretty cute in this uniform."

Time passed and I got a bit anxious. No cars were passing by. I saw a frog jumping toward a small lake to refresh. I guessed it would get very hot out there, so I picked up the frog to help. As I looked into its eyes, I thought I saw a reflection of someone but she jumped away before I could tell who it was.

Finally, the school bus! But it wouldn't stop. I reached out my hand to signal for it to stop. It looked the driver didn't even see me and I felt desperate, having waited so long. Another bus came along. This time, I wanted to make sure the driver saw me so I in the middle of the highway. It worked! The bus stopped and I got in.

The driver was very fat, like the frog I picked up earlier. He asked me to sit behind him. He was driving really fast. I could see the small town houses and beautiful venues whizzing by. A man on the bus asked him to stop, but he kept going so they started fighting. It got so crazy the door was pushed open and both of them fell out. Oh no, who is going to drive the bus? The children started freaking out. I thought to myself, "Great. I'm going to have to drive now." So I held the wheel and sat in the driver's seat, but I was too small for it and could barely see the road past the dashboard.

I tried to drive on, straight through trees and bushes. I drove through an empty house. Good thing it didn't get out of hand! I wanted to get to school much earlier but there was always something in the way. I drove so fast, the bus flew in the air a few times. I couldn't control my emotions. I couldn't explain it, but I liked it.

I saw the town we were supposed to stop in. The bus station was full and I couldn't find a place to park this thing. I let go of the wheel and told everyone to jump out of the windows. I jumped too, and hit the ground without pain. I got up and walked away, pretending nothing happened.

I saw a mall nearby so I crossed the street to check it out.

There were people going crazy over some shoes. I thought the shoes were very ugly so I took all of them away and cut them in half. I showed the people that this would stop the fighting. I laughed hard about it all.

Two good-looking men with guns passed by. They started shooting everyone. I hid behind a desk and looked for guns to shoot back. I found one and ran out with it. On the way, I saw people on the floor and wondered why they had been killed. Those guys were handsome, but mean looking.

Outside, I saw my car parked nearby. I hopped in and started driving. I was really late for school by now and wanted to get there badly. My friend was waiting for me! The school bus was still parked on the street. This was a small town, there weren't a lot of people around. So I decided to keep driving around until I passed by my childhood home. I could see houses and old cars driving kids to school, ready to start class. I was happy for the first time. I saw the church, then my school. I parked my car and asked for a hall pass to enter my class. The teacher hadn't started yet. I sat for a while and heard a voice say, "You don't belong in this class. Pack your things and I will see you at your house." I was so mad. All these things I went through for nothing!

I drove to my home, where my dad was drunk with a couple of people. I saw my mom getting out of a bus across the street from my beautiful, white house. I was feeling happy for a long time, but there was something else. I couldn't remember why I was there, or why I was going to school with my old teacher in my old classroom. The only thing I knew was a feeling I had when I was with my family. I was happy like never before.

LIVING UNDERWATER

01/01/2014

I saw a house in the forest, the only one there. It was almost falling apart, the rooms filled with sadness. Some family members were living there with me. The floors were mostly dirt and the kitchen cabinet doors were falling off, revealing food inside. Whatever was there was left by the previous family. The sofa was damaged by time and the front door barely worked. But we were all there, trying to survive some kind of disaster.

I was sitting on the old sofa when I decided to go out and see what was left of the world. I walked out and saw a pretty green forest on one side, but noticed the house was sitting on a tiny island floating around in the water. The first thing that crossed my mind was, how was I going to get home? I couldn't swim very well and saw a lot of sharks. I saw a man near the corner of the house fixing an old-looking boat. I walked over and asked if he needed help. He said, "No, I'm almost done. I have been fixing this boat for a while, but now we can cross the ocean with this old, crappy boat." I laughed and thought he was funny. Off we sailed into the deep, clear ocean. I saw many fish and dolphins along the way.

Finally, we get to the other side. What a surprise! The town was destroyed. People were living on top of floating houses and even underwater. They had to swim to get anywhere. I saw a school bus used as a raft, too. A friend was living there who was married with two children. A bridge crossed over to a small village where people were living. The bridge was only for rich people to use, but there was no point in using it. All the houses were floating on the water and people could swim across.

I crossed a wooden bridge and found myself on a pile of rocks in a corner. It was night time, but the moon made plenty of light reflecting off the water. It looked beautiful, but I felt sad people were living like this. It was weird I never saw any sharks in the water beneath me. We got to a piece of land where people worked hard to put vegetables and other plants in the ground. People were sweeping the dirt away. Everyone looked OK to me. At least they were alive and happy here.

I walked deeper into the small portion of land. A lady told me to get in the mud. This scared me because it looked as if it would suck me in, but before I could move she punched me. I fell into the mud and into another place. Everyone looked good, dressed up and drinking from fancy glasses. I thought it was nice enough but didn't want to stay, so I escaped. I got back to the place where I crossed the bridge.

I went to look for my friend and saw the house that was my hiding place. I could see it was falling apart, into the ocean. I went to my hiding place but it was gone. Everyone knew my house was falling apart, so I decided to start swimming under the water. To my surprise, I wasn't the only one. Most people were under there too, swimming to their destiny.

I saw a friend and asked if I could stay with him since my home was destroyed. He said OK. I saw an ex-boyfriend from many years ago who was with a woman he married. Their baby was on a little hut he had built on a small portion of the white sand. I said hello to his wife and held the beautiful baby in my arms. The wife didn't like this much, so I left. I only wanted to say hi since there were only a few people left I knew.

LOOKING FOR AN EXIT

08/05/2013

I was running around the city looking for a place to hide. I had twenty people on my back. In the beautiful, yet dark city I found myself trapped. I saw the time pass on my watch. Whoever was chasing me wanted me bad. The only thing holding me back was my true love who was still there but I couldn't get him back. He didn't have any idea what was happening in my life. I kept thinking of a place I could hide.

I entered a fancy restaurant. Wealthy people ate and had fun, looking at me like why is she running around here? I didn't care. I kept running until I passed the kitchen and saw a chef cutting up a rat for dinner. I asked, "What the fuck?" I kept going until I found a door marked EXIT. I found myself on a corner of a hill. I saw rocks along the river with an ugly, old bridge. The door was still open, and I looked back through it to see people with guns ready to shoot where I was standing.

I jumped over the rocks to cross to the other side. I heard my true love screaming my name from the other side. I thought to myself if I take one more step, I'll be there. But I forgot the people had guns and were shooting at me. I fell into the river, where the water was going down. The people shot at my back. I fell to my knees and looked for anything to protect myself. I found a gun but couldn't shoot it- I wasn't strong enough. I was bleeding too much from the bullets that were now lodged in my bones. The only word I said was, "Why?" I watched them surround me. If it were only one person, I could have easily escaped, but they knew I could fight so they all ganged up on me. With a sad face, I died.

My only exit was to wake up. I thanked God it was just a nightmare, but I found myself alone in bed without the love of my life.

MOUNTAIN HOUSE

11/27/2013

I sat on a big, white sofa and heard a doorbell. So I walked to the door and saw a white envelope sitting on the threshold. I picked it up and opened it. What a surprise! It was a white piece of paper with an address stamped in red ink. An old, red, '60s-style phone began to ring. I picked it up and heard an old man's voice say, "You've been invited to join us at a party we're having at the address your invitation mentioned. I will be waiting for you." He hung up, and I began to wonder if I should go.

I decided to attend and walked upstairs to my room to open a small, black suitcase. I took some white clothes from my closet and a few guns from under my bed. I went to the kitchen and grabbed some knives from a drawer, and put everything in the black suitcase. I opened a door that led to an old, dusty train station with no people around. I walked over and boarded a train that was waiting for me.

On the way, I traveled past a green forest with a river with lots of thick grass and trees as big as the dark sky. It looked beautiful and scary at the same time. I looked at my luggage and said, "Good thing I came prepared for the unknown."

Suddenly, the train stopped. I heard someone shout, "Here they come!" I looked to see a group of black horses running toward us. Their eyes were covered with red scarves. The horses stopped next to the train, one of them carrying a white paper in its mouth. The train conductor took the paper, read it, and gave it to me. He said, "It's for you, it has your name on it."

I didn't waste any time. I grabbed my luggage, jumped on the beautiful black horse, and took off to the mysterious address. We got close to a big mountain surrounded by mud. It looked like a giant mud man trying to stop me. One of the horses got trapped in the mud and started to sink into the earth. I reached for my suitcase, opened it, and took out a big knife. I cut the mud man in half with it.

We freed ourselves from the mud and rose fast until I arrived at the mysterious address. The house was on a mountain. There were trees inside, and the rest of the house was all wood. People were dressed up in very classic white clothes drinking red wine, and there were men in tuxedos escorting ladies by the arm.

A man opened the front door and showed me a room to rest and change in. I closed the door, took off my clothes, and changed into a long, white, beautiful dress. I came out of the room to join the crowd, but what a surprise! Everyone had turned into wolves and started eating each other.

As soon as they saw me, they wanted to eat me alive. My first reaction was to go back to the room and grab the guns I brought for the trip and kill them all. I hid next to the bed. A big tree led out to another small house. As I climbed onto it and into the other house, a wolf saw me and then all of them started running toward me.

I shot some, but a few still chased me as I got closer to the small house. The night was turning to day as the sun came up. The wolves were changing back to humans. As for me, I was still full of energy to kill them all. Then, I realized it was dangerous but I said to myself it was a good thing it was all just a dream.

48

MY FRIEND AND I

03/12/2013

It was a cloudy day when I saw my friend looking for me in a city with a railroad and lots of dying cornfields. I was just a girl running around with other strangers. We were running from someone we never saw, but the air felt cold and scary. I saw a house along a walkway. It had a store on the first floor with stairs leading up to what looked like a castle. It seemed abandoned. The cold air from outside was coming through the open windows. I felt cold and scared, so I decided to leave.

As I started running, I saw a car coming fast from the corner. The car stopped and I heard someone telling me to get in. It was a silver sedan. We drove around the city and stopped to pick someone up. We drove across the train tracks and saw homeless people quickly pushing shopping carts around. They were crossing the tracks to get to the other side, where there were narrow paths of dead corn plants and a body of water with long, green plants. Everyone was scared of the mysterious, cold spirit and running away from it.

I found myself walking with friends I knew in real life. One of them was a tall, black skinny man. He had on a white t-shirt and blue sweat pants, carrying a small bag around his neck. We were walking alone because everyone else had disappeared. So there we were, on a very narrow path heading toward a big, old, gray gate. For us, it felt like a safe place.

Right next to us, we could see the ocean. It was so close we could touch it. It was clear with green plants growing underneath. I looked again and saw the clear water was turning into petroleum. It looked like black gelatin, as if you could cut out a piece of it and take half of the ocean. We crossed over it easily. Finally, we got to the end of the narrow road. The creaky gate doors opened on their own, welcoming us.

We entered the gates and saw a white, two-story house surrounded by a large garden. My black friend sat in a chair, then his phone rang. Tears welled up in his eyes. I asked him what was wrong. He said, "My mother has died." We couldn't believe what we had just heard. I gave him a hug and walked around the house. I went upstairs and turned my head to a window, where two girls were making out on a bed. I walked forward but there was not much more to see. I went back downstairs into a hallway and saw two celebrities sitting and talking. I said hi, but they didn't reply so I walked away.

50

I went back upstairs and ended up on the roof. I was trying to leave that house, so I jumped up to fly away. Just then, my tall black friend called out my name. I jumped back and landed near him. He gave me his hand and we sat in a corner of the house. I held him and we looked away into the blue sky.

NIGHTMARE

06/24/1998

It was a beautiful night. The stars were lighting my way home as the breeze touched my face, pulling my long black hair back. The air smelled like mountain pines. I heard a noise from across the road. I looked around, but saw no one. I kept walking and saw my house a bit further away. I thought I should hurry because I wanted to get there fast. I saw a car with flowers head up the hill. I didn't think much about it and kept walking.

I saw people in front of my house carrying instruments to play. Inside, two of my brothers were playing around. I was seeing them as children, as if I went to visit my past where I was young, too. My mom told me, "Hurry and get dressed for church." I opened the door to my room and saw a black dress on the bed. I put it on and looked in the mirror.

I opened the door to leave the room but found myself in another place, with white snow and no one around. I asked myself, "How will I get to the church if nothing is around here?" I went back home, opened the door, and found myself up in the hills with many of the townspeople. I saw the car with the flowers. I didn't see my mom, so I asked a lady where she was.

"They already left. We already had the service," she said.

At that moment, I heard gunshots. I looked down the hill and saw some guys shooting up at the sky. I ran home to see if everyone was OK. I crossed a portion of farmland that only had black rows of tilled soil.

The wind was getting heavy. As I walked, I couldn't see very well. My feet were getting heavy, too. I looked at all the dirt on my shoes. I looked next to me to find a white coffin with some guy sleeping in white clothes. I looked close and saw it was my godfather from the time of my high school graduation. I felt sad. I thought about all those people up the hill in church and how the car with flowers was for him. I immediately ran home, scared.

I got to my room and turned on the light. I opened the curtains and saw my godfather walking toward my room. I was spooked and prayed he wouldn't hurt me. He knocked on my window, trying to get in. When I first saw his face, it made me sad. It became scary as he tried to break my window. I prayed to God and wanted to wake up when I heard the door open. It was my mom, who came to see what was happening.

I opened my eyes but was still in my dream. I told my mother about the dream. I woke up that day with a broken window.

PREGNANT IN MY DREAM

08/05/2013

I had a beautiful child with blond hair and beautiful brown eyes. From his big smile, you could tell how happy he was. We lived in my old hometown and were fairly happy, but there was a mystery surrounding me and my baby. I was worried the gods would come and take him away from me. As I was walking on the road to a nearby town to visit a friend of mine, I felt like my stomach was growing bigger, getting hard. It was dark and all I could see was the road. I saw some rocks, bushes, and trees, along with old wood houses.

As I got closer to my friend's house, horses were running on the side of the road and people were running in slow motion. I had to cross a row of beautiful, brown wheat fields. I heard something like a gunshot. I looked over and saw two men fighting, but I kept walking. I finally arrived at my friend's home. She had a husband I felt like I knew from another place, but I wasn't sure.

She was outside hanging some clothes, and he was inside folding more clothes. It was dark inside and I could only see the light blue walls. It was a mess in there. Clothes were everywhere! I felt my stomach turning. I looked at it and saw it was getting big, as if I was pregnant. I told the woman's husband that perhaps I was pregnant but he didn't want to hear it. I didn't mind too much because I thought it was a weird thing to say to him, anyway.

As I left the house, I heard someone say, "The gods are here to take your baby and kill him." I got scared. I didn't want them to take my child, or the baby on the way. I started running and felt the weight in my stomach as I looked down at my colorful, flower-print dress. I found some friends along the way; they had guns. We got to the garden outside my house. I looked up. The sky opened and I saw three men on horseback ride down toward us. One man was wearing a dress and carrying a magic wand, the other two carried whips. They were after me and my son.

My baby was in the garden, near me. I didn't know what to do. They looked powerful and I didn't have any powers at that time. One of them took my son. I tried to get closer but the man in the dress threw a lasso around my body as if I were an animal. I tried to fly, but couldn't. He pulled me around while riding the horse. They didn't want me to save my beautiful child. I got really mad and tried hard to get the rope off my body.

I had more friends who came to rescue me. I started screaming, "Leave my baby alone!" The three men surrounded him as I grew angrier. It was as if I was living that moment in reality. I picked up strength and ran toward them. I took my child, held him, and tried to leave, but found myself in another place. I was in a building with an elevator that had a bed next to it. I hid my baby under the bed. The gods were inside the elevator looking for us. Some friends helped us escape that place, but the gods were still looking for us. I couldn't let them kill my child for no reason. I was wondering why they wanted him. We hid in a house I always found in my dreams. It had a tunnel with doors leading to old rooms deep within. We hid there as my stomach grew big. I almost gave birth in that house. I felt safe.

SCARY ME

11/25/2013

The store was in Mexico City, on the corner of a hill. The street next to the store was dark and scary, and no one was outside. Only dogs barked. I rushed to the store from my home, walking down the dark city street. Dogs were trying to get out of their houses to bite me. They were angry like they were hungry; hungry for blood. My first reaction was to walk faster until I got to the store. Finally, I got to the front door. No one was there and the door was locked.

I crossed the street. I saw a hospital with wide doors. I kept looking inside to see what was moving around in there, and suddenly saw a man. He pulled me inside the hospital with big, scary hands and closed the doors. He took me to a room I had been to before. I didn't remember much about that time except for the bed, the sheets, and a picture of a saint on the floor. I picked it up to look at it and said, "There you are, old saint picture." I walked over to hang it on the wall.

An old lady sat close to the empty wall. I got scared for a second. I moved closer to her and saw her face. It was my grandma, sitting in an old chair. She asked, "Why did it take you so long?"

"I thought you were at the corner store," I answered. Grandma pointed at the bed. I saw my daughter laying there. I held her in my arms and said, "What are you doing here? You don't belong. Go back home."

My daughter opened her eyes and said, "We are trapped in this room with you, Grandma." We heard steps coming from the hallway. I touched the wall and laid there for a moment. A man opened the door, looked around, and then closed it. I opened the window and took my Grandma and daughter away from that crazy room.

The man returned, but this time I escaped by hanging on his back like a ghost. He opened the outside door and I jumped into a car full of blankets from the hospital. The car drove away and I looked around at this poor city with its garbage on the streets, dilapidated houses, and rusty old cars. Smoke was everywhere, the sky was cloudy. I saw a small, blue car. My sister was driving around with my mother, daughter and Grandma. I jumped out of the car filled with blankets and ran fast toward the blue car. I felt like someone was following me, turned my head to look, but no one was there. I couldn't fit my body in the car. It was tiny, and too many people were inside. Only my feet and half my body were in, but I told my sister to drive fast.

We left that poor city. It was getting dark and my sister stopped the car. She said, "Here we are."

I saw white, sandy mountains with people holding candles. Some of them had blood on them. I asked, "Where the fuck are we?"

SNAKES IN MY DREAMS

11/03/2013

It was dark that day. There were damaged, brown buildings and the streets were empty, no sign of humans. Across the street was a fenced park, and at the corner was a river of water. The river was strange looking. On my way I saw a friend of mine. I asked him if he was there for the same reason. He said, "Yes, I will help you fight it." We walked through a door and wound up in my apartment. I found it funny to discover my ex-husband there, along with a few other people. I couldn't see who they were. I think they all wanted to live there, because they hung out for a long time and didn't want to leave.

I opened a door to a room. I opened another one and found myself in a green garden with lush grass and tall trees. It was hard to get in there, so I went back to my apartment. I asked my ex why all those people were in my home. He was on the phone, but I'm not sure who he was talking to. I went back to my own room but instead wound up in the garden. I saw snakes hanging from the trees, trying to bite me. I grabbed one by the neck and killed her. Suddenly, I was walking next to a man I thought I knew. I held his hand, and he told me he would help me fight the snakes.

We left the house. As we were walking out, I looked back to see my home covered in a big, brown metal fence. I said to myself, "That's why they wanted to live here. It's safe." But I was back on the streets to get to the river and kill snakes for them, so they could live happily in my home. I could come back to my house with no worries in my head.

I got to the river, which was clear with green plants and lots of snakes under the surface. All kinds of different snakes were swimming around. One had a long, green body; the one that really worried me looked like a dragon with the face of an old man. It was slithering toward me. I was thinking I couldn't mess with this one. She was old and big and could kill me at any moment. I kept walking slowly and quietly, without fear. I went back home and said, "I can't kill the snakes."

DEATH GIRL

03/13/2014

It was very dark. I could barely see where I was walking, but I knew I was headed home. I saw a little house without any windows, only a wooden door that was falling apart. Just as I passed by, I heard the voice of a little girl. I thought she needed help, so I opened the door. As soon as I entered, I felt cold and my skin began to crawl. There was nothing but white mud and a couple of chairs in the corner. I walked further inside and saw mud draining through the hole.

I got scared and walked out of the house. But I heard the girl's voice again. I ran home and saw two men and two women drinking wine together. My heart was racing, I couldn't take it. They were waiting for me to leave town. I told them to wait outside while I grabbed my daughter. They waited for me at the bus stop. I woke up my daughter and left the house.

We all waited for the bus to show up when suddenly the girl's voice cried out again. We all stared at the house I was just in. The men wanted to look around but I told them not to go because it was dangerous. I had already been in to look and no one was there. It was an empty house full of white mud, sand, and a hole in the corner. They didn't want to hear it and walked back to check it out. The bus was coming. I didn't think twice, leaving with the two women and my daughter on the bus. All I could think about was the house and the girl's voice. What happened to her?

We arrived and I left my daughter in an unfamiliar house. I just wanted to keep her in a safe place. I came outside to see the house we had escaped from- right next to us! It was so strange. I kept walking. I saw people with drinks and heard music all around. It was a big birthday celebration. I asked the two women about the two men. They said they hadn't returned yet. Right away, I felt something was wrong. I needed to go back there. I went to look for a car, but they were hard to find. I walked back to the house and saw the men in there. I asked them why they were taking so long. They said there was a little girl who was dead and they wanted to bury her in another place. They took her out of a hole. The house was moving like there was an earthquake. A giant hole was opening in that house. I ran out with the men and found ourselves back at my old house.

Walking up to the hills, I saw a girl flying across the mud fields, screaming. We looked to see she was dripping with blood. I felt an invisible force holding me back. I couldn't see and I couldn't cry out; I was totally paralyzed. All the other people were walking backwards to the house.

I saw a tree and held myself to it. As I got stronger, I stood and walked back to the house to fight that thing. As I entered the house, I saw her cutting the men apart. I saw blood everywhere and a leg flew by. I grabbed rocks to throw but nothing happened. She was getting closer and closer. My father appeared, and helped me to defeat the girl who was either possessed or dead. Crazy.

I woke up barely able to breathe, like there was a very heavy weight on my chest.

THE HANDSOME GUY SHARING THE SOFA

06/30/2013

Inside a penthouse apartment next to the ocean, I was living with a stranger who was sharing the sofa with me. I walked to the kitchen to grab a soda. The kitchen was wide open with no windows, and the walls were made of wood. I could see the beautiful ocean. I tried to fix wood that was falling away from the walls, but couldn't. I didn't have time. A big storm was coming from the coast. I felt attached to the stranger, as if we were connected somehow. I heard people on the street yelling, "It's coming to get us! Run, hide, until you die!" As I tried to leave the kitchen, I could see giant waves ready to wash over us all.

The ocean had morphed into a big, mad, hungry mouth. I held my breath and clutched a metal pole underwater. I saw people washing away, passing me by. I was terrified and wanted to wake up but couldn't. I wasn't able to hold my breath for long. I felt a hand grab mine and pull me up to a ship that looked very old and only had a deck left to it.

It was raining. I opened my eyes and found myself with others who had survived the catastrophe. A little blond girl, still in the water, was crying out for help. She nearly drowned. The water swelled halfway up all the buildings of the city.

I quickly swam over to grab her hand, and took her to the only ship left. I rescued her from death. Rivers of dirty water where streets used to be were all I could see. My memories brought me back to a party I attended on a rooftop, where women danced in nice dresses. I heard music coming from upstairs. I spoke with beautiful people I had never seen before.

A few hours later, I left with a handsome guy. I felt like I knew him, but his face wasn't familiar. It was the same guy who shared the sofa with me, the same man who rescued me from the ocean floor- he was with me now, and we were looking for a way to survive together. We navigated the rivers that took over the city. We searched for dry land to stop and live on. We didn't see anything. Only people screaming for help from the flooded buildings. We decided to rescue them before it was too late.

THE MOON AND THE GORILLA

It was dark in the city, the white moon illuminating the streets. An old, rusty building had nothing inside but darkness. No one was out except me. A black gorilla appeared, half wolf with long teeth and hairy all over. He was chasing me around. I didn't know what he wanted from me. The only thing I knew is that he was scary, and right at my back. I saw stairs leading up to a building. I ran to them and climbed them until I got to the roof, close to the moon. I could almost touch it, but didn't want to waste time. The gorilla jumped up to the roof as well, so I ran fast from building to building trying to escape. He was so close he almost grabbed my arm, but I jumped up to another building.

He did the same but didn't make it and fell down to the ground.

I looked down and there he was, maybe dead or just pretending. I was finally alone without fear. I decided to come down the stairs and walk to the nearest train station. I boarded a train that took me to the next village, between the mountains. On the way, the only thing I saw was the moon following me. It was dark and cold outside; I could see the wind touching the windows as my breath made condensation on them. My thought was how did I get there and why was this big, ugly gorilla chasing me?

I needed to find an answer. Finally, the train stopped at the village. I walked out and kept going, straight to the street. I saw some farmers cultivating flowers in the muddy earth. I asked them if there were wolves or any type of monsters around, or if anyone was hurt by them. One said, "No. Over here, we just work in the land. Go home, little girl." I walked away and crossed fields of flowers. They were green and long. It was still dark, and I just wanted to be home. I saw the farmers running toward me. I looked and there he was! This gorilla was after everyone. They got to where I was standing so I ran until I got to the edge of a mountain. Nothing was out there but mountains. I felt trapped and scared. The more time I spent figuring out how I could jump, the closer he got. These poor farmers were being killed by the gorilla, so I felt I had to fight it. But how if I had no weapons?

There was only grass, flowers, and trees around. I jumped down. As I fell down the mountain, I felt my stomach twist and turn. The worst feeling was when I was about to hit the ground. My feet were tingling. It was the worst feeling ever. Then, I looked up. The sky was opening and a bunch of stars were twinkling. The clouds were moving around fast. I flew up to the open sky to leave that place between the stars.

THE TSUNAMI

02/28/2012

I was standing on top of a house when I heard someone scream, "Run fast up to the hills, the storm is coming!" I saw no one running on those green mountains. My first thought was to find my family. I decided to walk on a gray pathway to search for them. As I walked, two men started walking close to me. They came from out of nowhere; they were wearing old clothes, from the 14th century. They had big guns ready to fire, and came to hunt me down. I started running fast until I lost them. Looking to the sky, I saw it was getting dark and the rain was falling hard.

I touched my face to wipe the drops from my eyes. Slowing down, I almost fell on the slippery road. My hand grabbed something at my side; a big, brown wall. I wiped my eyes again to see clearly and walk around the wall. It was a big, fancy hotel. I found the front entrance and stepped onto the patio. I was just in time to see big waves coming from an angry lake.

One of my sisters stepped out from the hotel, which I thought was strange. I asked her, "Where is the rest of our family?"

She said, "They are not here, only me. But look at the cloudy, dark sky. The storm is coming and there is no place to hide."

She ran back inside. I stayed there, in a state of shock. I watched and felt the earth moving- it was a big boat coming in with strong waves pulling it along. It was so close, I could touch it with my hands as it came up to destroy half of the land. I felt a strong wind blowing me into the water. Scared, I closed my eyes and held on to a pole with all my might. I found myself under the waves, which were now swallowing everything in their path. In the blink of an eye, the waves subsided and the water was calm. Everything was destroyed, the roads were turned into water and the hotel was halfway in the lake. As I carefully made my way up a straight path on the hill, I see boats cut in half, people floating, and alligators ready to attack. I see a child crying for his life so I jumped in the water to rescue him. I took his hand, pulling him out and leaving him on the side. An alligator clamped down on my arm and dragged me to the water, so I punched him hard until I won the fight. A man pulled me up fast, then carried me on the dry road. Finally, more land! He put me in the seat of a Jeep, started the car and drove fast. I saw more soldiers helping survivors. The man who rescued me was a soldier. I asked him, "Where is my family?"

"They are waiting for you on the other side," he said, "but for now take this gun. We have a big fight- the bad guys want to take the only town left, and we need to bring the survivors to get food and shelter."

I saw the two guys who wanted to hunt me down earlier, riding in another car. They were going to this small town to take all they wanted. I shoot them all with the gun and finally we win the war of the tsunami! At that moment, I woke up.

THE WOMAN IN BLACK

09/04/2013

I found myself back at my parents' house with some friends. We were drinking outside next to the red and blue roses my mom planted in her garden that afternoon. There was darkness in the air. We didn't care since we were drinking and having a good time like the old days, playing spin the bottle. The bottle went around and around until it was my turn, but I let it go because I didn't want to kiss my friend's boyfriend at that moment.

I didn't have a partner then. My mom told me it was getting dark and we needed to leave the house because she was going out, and no one would be there to protect us. We all went in the house and sat on the floor. Suddenly, the earth moved beneath us. It was an earthquake. We got scared and left the room, heading to the second floor where we felt safe.

As time passed, we wanted to leave but couldn't because it was really dark out. I could barely see my hands in front of my face. The light suddenly went out with a booming sound. We looked out the windows and didn't see anything because it was so dark. We decided to make the best of it and we all made up beds with lots of blankets. Then we were in the kitchen, talking about being hungry and there was nothing to eat.

Suddenly, someone knocked on the door really hard three times. Who could it possibly be at this time of night? No one wanted to open the door. I decided to open it myself, and what a surprise! It was my friend. He said some guy had pushed him and he landed outside the house, so he didn't think twice about knocking hard. I welcomed him with a hug, and we walked to the second floor where the rest of us were staying.

Everyone had their phones off. The only light came from burning candles. We heard a noise downstairs again. I didn't want to move from where I was laying. Someone got up to check it out, but never returned. Then the house started moving again, so violently this time that the windows almost shattered. I went downstairs. I felt someone behind me trying to touch me. I almost peed my pants! It was such a cold and scary feeling. I screamed my friend's name. Right away, he came to see what was happening. When I saw his face, I also saw a lady dressed in black with a veil covering her face, looking at him. She stared at me. I told my friend to stay still, there was a lady on his back.

He looked back and saw the lady, who told us it was time to eat. We ran out of the house and I found myself in another place with a lot of light.

UNSOLVED CASE

01/02/2010

I was driving my tiny car in a neighborhood with houses that all looked the same. They were white, with green garbage cans, and mailboxes outside. The streets were somewhat narrow and very clean. A couple of ladies were walking with dogs, and an old guy crossed in front of my car. He looked at me with a mean face, but I ignored him. My mission was to find the beach and meet a guy that had a video showing an Indian man's death.

The drive was frustrating because I couldn't go very fast and my brakes didn't work. Another man was crossing the street as I tried to stop my car, but couldn't. The brakes were gone and I was really scared I would hit him, so I rolled down my window and told him to move fast. But oh boy, the guy was too old to move fast enough. I felt my leg push hard into the brake pedal, but nothing. Good thing my car slowed down in time for him to cross the road.

In this community, I could see a big building with the beach nearby, but for some reason I couldn't get there. I drove around in circles. I stopped my car to walk, which seemed better as I was getting nowhere. I parked on the side of the street and walked to the beach. It was getting dark. I heard a couple arguing in the house next door. Their lights were on and the windows were wide open. I thought it was a nice house. I kept walking down, but wasn't getting any closer to the beach. I asked a lady how to get there. She told me, "Only you can, if you have a soul." I thought that was weird and kept walking.

Finally, I was getting closer but not enough. I could see I was still far away. I took my car and drove. Why not drive there? I get there and park the car. Three guys are on the corner watching me from a parking lot near the calm beach water in front of me. There was a small hill of big, green bushes next to me I had to get through to meet this guy. I jumped through, opening the bushes. I had made my way to another beach. Everyone was happy there. I saw girls in bikinis, guys in the water and guys on shore making some barbecue. As I walked, a girl touched my shoulder and said, "The old guy is there. Go talk to him. Hurry, because it's getting dark." I got close to him and he said hi to me. He looked happy.

The old man said, "Here is the video. Watch it. I will put it right on this TV." They had TVs on the beach! I watched the video of an Indian guy getting killed from behind. His body was naked and fit, a chicken feather in his hair. A man walked behind him and choked him to death. As he was dying, I saw he was staring at me and pointing at something with a wooden stick in his hand. He started scratching at the floor as he was choked.

I decided to take the video home to analyze it closely. As I walked, the three guys were getting close.

My friend the old guy sent his big dogs to chase them as I crossed through the bushes to get back to my car. There was a man waiting for me, one of my friends. He told me to change my clothes, so I put on a red suit and white pants. I told him I loved my red suit. He said I looked great. Suddenly, a TV was on top of my head with the video playing. I was thinking it was a clue.

We entered into a very dark place to investigate. I couldn't see very well. The only thing I could see was a mound of white powder in a bowl and wooden sticks, like the one I saw in the video. I had found a clue, but steps came toward us. I got scared and grabbed a stick. A word appeared in the powder. It was YOU. I put more powder down and more words appeared. It said YOU KILL YOU. Then, the footsteps came close to me. I got really scared. I tried to wake up. Good thing I heard a noise in my home that did actually wake me. Case unsolved.

WHITE SHINY DRESS

07/07/2013

At a restaurant made to look like a castle from long ago, up the hill from a village, there I was dressed up in a white silk dress sitting at a table. I was with some girls I didn't know, but they were also dressed up nice. We were drinking tea in white cups and eating slices of chocolate cake I brought there with the few dollars I had left in my purse. I got up and looked at the cake, wanting to eat more. I opened my purse and searched for more money, but I didn't have any. The girls were dancing around the table. They looked happy, so I thought it was a good time to leave them.

Someone called my phone and said, "It was important." I was walking downstairs from the restaurant. A silver truck was waiting for me out front, which I thought was weird. In an instant, I was sitting in the truck and could see my mom's house. I had the phone in my hand when it started ringing again. It was my mom, so I answered. She asked me to get food from down the hill. I started the truck and drove off, thinking of my money. Where did it go, and how could I buy food if I didn't have enough to pay?

I stopped in front of a restaurant that was supposed to serve my mom's food. I got out and walked closer. I looked down at my dress. It was changing colors; from blue to red, and then back to white like it was before. I kept walking to the stairs. There was a guy who looked homeless, eating outside.

I went in and ordered food, but instead they gave me cake. The few dollars in my purse was not enough to get the chocolate cake. I walked downstairs and asked a man eating steak to let me borrow some money. I told him to hurry up. I didn't want anyone to see that. The guy lent me $20. It was good enough.

I went back to pay, and sat waiting for the food or cake at a table covered in white satin. The girls I was with earlier from the other restaurant were there, and the same things were around the room. They liked my white dress and gave me a veil. I put in on and with much joy, we ran around the table and said, "This is my white veil."

I was tired and ready to go home. My sister called and my phone rang like a bell. I ran with the food to my mom's house on the dark streets. I found myself on the corner. There was a man who grabbed my hand and tried to take my dress off. I screamed my lungs out until someone heard me. A man sleeping on the second floor of an apartment with his lights on and the window open heard me.

I saw him in his bed, and he went to the window to look at us. He jumped down to us, punched the man in the face, and took me inside his home.

There were people there who knew me from the restaurant. They told me to be careful, because the devil was outside the doors. I wanted to go, still carrying the food my mom asked me to get. I told the guy to take me home. I would fight the devil that was on the streets. We couldn't leave him out there because he would hurt others. We took a van and some guns. The guy was nice. He did everything he could to keep me safe. We passed through dark streets and up hills, but didn't find the devil. Finally, I got home and my mom was happy to see me and her food. I looked at my dress; it was still white and clean. I woke up hungry that day.

WOLVES IN MY DREAMS

09/23/2006

I found myself feeling lonely in a place full of people. They were having fun, drinking heavily. They had full glasses of liquor in their hands, but I was just there watching them. I saw how they were falling down and wasting their money. I talked to one of them, but it seemed like he didn't hear me, so I sat down on a sofa. There was someone sitting there who looked at me like I was doing something wrong just being there. It felt like everyone was against me for no reason, so I left for the beach.

It was a beautiful night, full of stars that lit up the sky. I could see the white sand and the clear ocean reflecting the stars above. I was feeling calm, relaxed. I needed peace, so I stayed off to the side. Far away, I saw a lot of people running. They were coming my way. They passed by me, but couldn't see me, so I just continued to stand and watch. They were scared to death. I could see it in their faces. They were carrying knives and things to defend themselves. Then, I saw wolves. Their fur was white and brown; their teeth were long, pointy, and sharp. They were ready to attack and bite anybody. When I looked again, the people disappeared. It was just me and the wolves.

I ran to hide on top of a little sand dune. I waited there for the wolves to leave, but they didn't go anywhere. They were on the edge of the beach waiting for me. I wanted to leave so badly. I looked around for an escape route and saw nothing but the beach, dotted with small bushes. I was getting sleepy but had to stay awake. Those wolves would eat me! I looked again and from far away, I could see the top of a little Tiki house. Since I was dressed in white, it was easy for me to lie on the white sand and drag myself to the little house unnoticed. I got up from the little dune to check what the wolves were doing, but they were just lying there with their eyes open.

I saw a few more people running from more wolves. They were following them closely. It was my chance to leave! I ran as fast as I could to get to the Tiki house. I lay there for a minute. I heard someone scream. I looked out the window and saw a concrete house with a woman inside, screaming. I didn't see any wolves around, just her. I thought it would be a good place to hide, better than the Tiki house. If they get here, they can easily destroy it. I looked to see if there were any weapons around to defend myself, but there was nothing. Just a couple of long, wood sticks. I sharpened them.

The wolves were getting closer. They could smell me. I had to hurry, they were wild and hungry. I checked to see if the sunrise was coming, but it was still dark. I grabbed the sharp sticks and walked to the concrete house. On the way, two wolves were waiting for me. I fought them, one pushing me to the sand and trying to bite. I saw blood in his open mouth, left over from the last kill. I got strong and pushed him away; he was hurt and left me alone. The other tried to attack me, but I ran fast and got to the door of the concrete house.

I tried to get in but couldn't. Someone saw me trying to open the door. Several wolves had gathered together to attack me. Two men showed up out of nowhere and helped me fight them. The screaming girl from earlier in the dream opened the door for us as we fought the wolves. More were coming! We got inside and locked the door. We hid in the house to try and survive, waiting for the sun to rise.

ZOMBIE TOWN

01/22/2013

I was with a few friends at a funeral in a cemetery. The man who passed away was a friend of ours. While standing there, I saw the sky was clear and the grass was green. It was such a beautiful day for such a sad passing. We watched the burial. We left and walked across the street. Our house was a base for planes and ships we could fly into space. The ships looked like large balls, with some regular airplane parts on them. Everything was secure.

My bed was next to my friend's bed. I was about to fall asleep when I heard screaming outside. I got up and checked outside my window. I saw a couple of people standing and looking at the cemetery we buried my friend in. I decided to go to them and find out why they were there. On the way was a playground. I saw a few of them on the swing set. Their moms were sitting on the grass, watching. I thought that was cute.

I came across some people gathered around my friend's grave. Suddenly, my dead friend rose from his grave! My first reaction was to find a stick and hit his head a few times, but he just got up and started chasing me around with a very scary face. I figured it was the end times. My friend had turned into an ugly, dirty zombie and wanted to hunt me down. I ran and tried not to look back, but I had to. I felt as if his hand was going to grab my back. I turned to see his dog trying to bite me. I kicked it, hard. The dog flew away in pieces. I passed by the playground and saw the mothers biting their children. I felt bad, but at that moment I had to keep running for my life without any weapons to defend anyone, including myself.

I ended up in a very dark neighborhood where I could only see houses and people running for their lives. The zombies were everywhere. I saw a couple of men going into a house, the only one with lights on. I ran up and a zombie with scary eyes and a rotting head stopped me.

I thought if I hit him in the head like I had seen in movies, he might die. So I punched him until he fell to the ground, and I kicked him really hard.

People were running around like crazy and would just smash the zombies with their feet. I got to the house, jumped on the roof, and snuck up to a window to see what was happening. The men were so drunk they didn't care. I hid under the bed and waited for them to leave. I heard the door open and saw a lady walking calmly toward a bed to hide under as the men drank beer in the kitchen. I went to the door and knocked a few times. It was dark. I looked around for any zombies, but they were busy eating people on the street. The lady opened the door, and I told her to let me stay there for the night. She said OK and told me to come in. I told her to lock the windows and turn off the lights, but she didn't want to hear it. She sat with the men and started drinking with them.

I was terribly scared, so I went back to the room to find a bed to sleep in and think of all this as just a nightmare. I heard a noise. I opened the bedroom door and saw two zombies coming in through the window! The men were still drunk and still did not care. I hid under the bed and waited for them to leave. I heard the door open and saw the lady trying to hide under the other bed, but the zombies managed to take her and rip her apart. I watched blood pooling on the floor. I wanted to leave; I needed to escape the house, but could hear zombies on the roof, pounding and scraping around. My only way out was the window, so I grabbed a silver rod from the bed frame and calmly struck the zombie who was eating the woman's remains. Yuck, it was gross.

I looked around and saw a couple of my friends trying to save me. I screamed, "I'm here!" They threw me a big gun. I shot the zombies in my way. It was so dark I could barely see. I got a bit scared but was comforted by the thought of getting home safe, and couldn't lose my faith that the sun would come up and everything would go back to normal. A zombie lady approached me, grabbing my hair and pulling it hard. I got really mad and whacked her with the gun in my hands. She was a little stronger than me, so she grabbed my hand and tried to bite it with her bloody mouth. I managed to pull her to the floor and kick her head. I ran home. On the way, I saw many people turn into zombies. I thought it was the end of this beautiful world!

When I finally got home, my friends were waiting for me to get to the ship and go to another planet. I put on some space clothes, jumped in a ship, and navigated out of the house. By that time it was daylight; I saw all the people far below on the ground running around like ants as we were leaving.

Maria Palomino was born in the heart of Mexico City, to a large family with 14 siblings. At age nine, Maria and her family moved to a small town away from city life. After high school Maria relocated to Miami where she now resides with her daughter and little dog, enjoying everything that South Florida has to offer her. After various careers and many tough times, Maria discovered her true passion to write and entertain people with her experiences, many of which are in the form of dreams.